Never be afraid to ask a question, especially of yourself. Discovery is the mission of life.
—Brian Kates

These are the days of miracle and wonder

D0574330

Computers are useless. They can only give you answers.
—Pablo Picasso

There really aren't just seven wonders of the world—there are more like seven million.
—Kobi Yamada

ever wonder

ask questions and live into the answers.

written by kobi yamada
designed by steve potter

COMPENDIUM™
INCORPORATED

live inspired.

ACKNOWLEDGEMENTS

This book is dedicated to all the seekers in life...may you always wonder and wander. Thank you for the inspiration.

WITH SPECIAL THANKS TO

Jason Aldrich, Gloria Austin, Gerry Baird, Jay Baird, Neil Beaton, Josie Bissett, Laura Boro, Jim and Alyssa Darragh & Family, Jennifer and Matt Ellison & Family, Rob Estes, Michael and Leianne Flynn & Family, Sarah Forster, Jennifer Hurwitz, Heidi Jones, Carol Anne Kennedy, June Martin, Jessica Phoenix and Tom DesLongchamp, Janet Potter & Family, Diane Roger, Kirsten and Garrett Sessions, Kristel Wills, Clarie Yam and Erik Lee, Heidi Yamada & Family, Justi and Tote Yamada & Family, Bob and Val Yamada, Kaz and Kristin Yamada & Family, Tai and Joy Yamada, Anne Zadra, August and Arline Zadra, Dan Zadra, and Gus and Rosie Zadra.

CREDITS

Written by Kobi Yamada
Designed by Steve Potter

ISBN: 978-1-888387-55-1

6th Printing. 10K 09 08
Printed in China

Have patience with everything unresolved in your heart

and try to **love the questions** themselves as if they were locked rooms

or books written in a very foreign language. **Don't search for the answers,**

which could not be given to you now, because you would not be able to live them.

And the point is to live everything.

Live the questions now. Perhaps then, some day far in the future,

you will gradually, without even noticing it,

live your way into the answer.

—Rainer Maria Rilke

ever wonder = wonder forever

The quality of your life is in direct proportion to the quality of the questions you ask yourself. Questions have tremendous power. If you want better answers for your life, ask better questions. Become aware of your own self-talk. Where do you put your attention? Questions are the source of life-enriching change. Your focus creates your reality. Whatever you are experiencing in life is not based on life itself but what you are focusing on. What you focus on increases.

If you want to change your reality, change your focus. If you want to change your focus, change the questions you ask yourself. Questions control your focus, therefore questions control your own experience of life. Thinking is nothing but the process of asking and answering questions. Instead of asking: "Why me?" "Why am I so unhappy?" "What's wrong with me?" Try asking: "How can I make this work?" "How can I make a difference?" "What am I grateful for?"

Whatever you ask for, you will get an answer. If you want a great life, ask great questions. Questions should empower you. You should ask a question with genuine expectancy and intention. Good questions are catalysts. They are challenges, inspirations, road maps, hints of something better, calls to action and new beginnings. *Ever Wonder* will give you a jump start, fresh eyes and inspiring questions to reflect on, ponder, consider and discuss with friends. Life is a self-fulfilling prophecy and seldom do we exceed our expectations. So get to know yourself, have fun, stretch your boundaries, be inquisitive and live your life on purpose.

What are you waiting for?

wonder forever

When was the last time

you did something for the first time?

What do you want from life?

In order to find yourself, are you

willing to lose yourself?

If you think life is hard, what are you

comparing it to?

What do you pack to pursue a dream

and what do you leave behind?

Why be afraid of

something you want?

Are you the type of person

with whom you would

like to spend the rest of your life?

Do you

know that today is your day?

If you don't think highly of yourself,

who will?

Is it true that you have to see it to

or rather, do you have

believe it,
to believe it before you can see it?

Do you realize that

nothing is too good to be true?

If you don't have all the things you
are you grateful for all the things

want,

you don't have that you didn't want?

Do you doubt your doubts?

What would you attempt

if you knew you could not fail?

What difference does it make if
the thing you're scared of

is real or not?

Do you know

how to dream with your eyes open?

If not now, when?

How would you introduce yourself to

God?

Do you know where you

are on your journey?

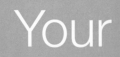
Your

destiny is coming, are you ready?

Can you really live life without loving
and can you love life

life
without living life?

Do you know that you are the one

you've been waiting for?

What is your unrelenting passion?

Do you let yesterday

use up too much of today?

Where does adventure live?

When will you ever have more time

than you do right now?

What are the five things you value

most in life?

Do you treat

love as a noun or a verb?

What is the one thing you think of

that always makes you smile?

Can you really be brave if
you've only had wonderful

things happen to you?

If what's in your dreams wasn't how could you even dream it?

already inside of you

Do you know that you know

far more than you know you know?

What good has worrying ever done?

How old would you be if

you didn't know how old you were?

Who are "they" that hold so much

power over our lives?

Have you begun today

what you wish to be tomorrow?

Do you have enough risks in your life

to stay alive?

Are you making new mistakes or the

same old ones?

Do you live from the

inside out or the outside in?

What would you think about if you

were not taught what to think about?

Are you

living a life of action or reaction?

If you give all your love away,

what do you have left?

Have you

discovered your mission in life?

If you're not happy with
what you have,

everything in your life right now…
and then somehow got them back?

What makes something beautiful?

Is it really always better to be safe

than sorry?

How do you find happiness?

Where do you draw the line

between possible and impossible?

Do you love everybody you love?

How

do you nurture your soul?

Are you willing to

continually dance with life?

How do you want to

be remembered?

What if you looked for the good in

everyone and in every situation?

Will you ever really

know how brave you truly are?

How far would you go to chase

what you really want?

How many ways do you

know to free yourself?

If you had five minutes to live,

who would you call

and why are you waiting?

Is not every end a new beginning?

What if the rest of your life

was the best of your life?

Maybe we should start

over from scratch…where is scratch?

ABOUT THE AUTHOR

Kobi Yamada makes his home in Seattle, Washington. He is the President/CEO of Compendium, Incorporated, one of the nation's top designers of inspirational gifts and books and a leading publishing and strategic communications company consulting high-profile organizations, including several Fortune 500 companies.

Anything is a wonder. It is not merely a world of miracles; it is a miraculous world.
—G.K. Chesterton

It is not the answer that enlightens, but the question.
—Eugene Ionesco

Have patience with everything unresolved in your heart and try to love the questions themselves.
—Rainer Maria Rilke

The more I wonder...the more I love.
—Alice Walker